IMAGES
of England

AROUND
GRANTHAM

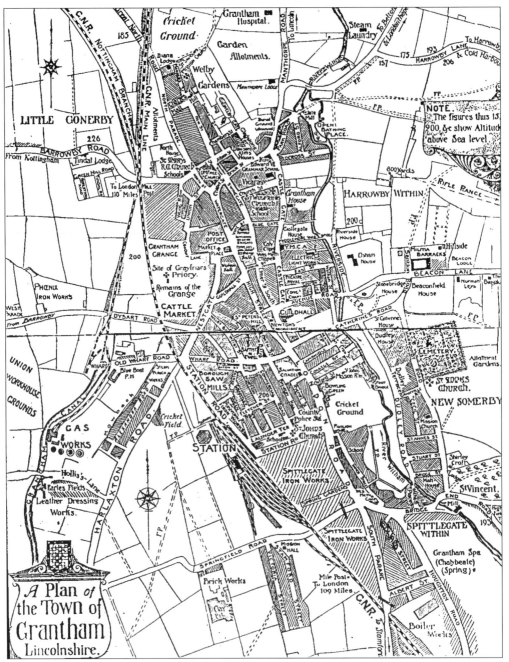

Map of Grantham, c. 1905.

IMAGES
of England

AROUND
GRANTHAM

Compiled by
Fred Leadbetter

TEMPUS

First published 2000
Copyright © Fred Leadbetter, 2000

Tempus Publishing Limited
The Mill, Brimscombe Port,
Stroud, Gloucestershire, GL5 2QG

ISBN 0 7524 1863 7

Typesetting and origination by
Tempus Publishing Limited
Printed in Great Britain by
Midway Clark Printing, Wiltshire

Contents

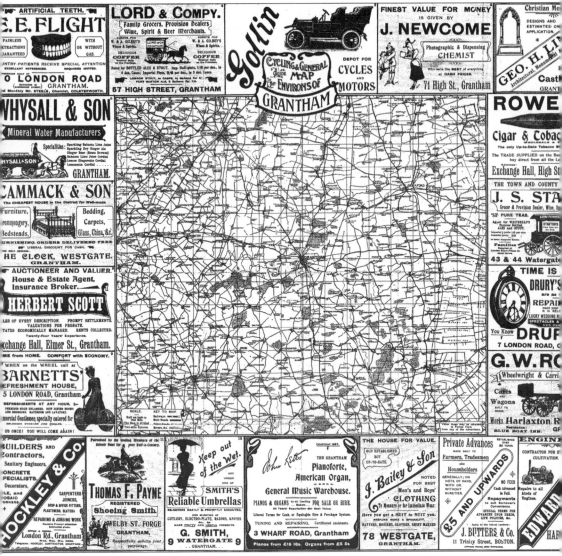

An Edwardian cyclists' map of the Grantham area, complete with local advertisements.

Introduction

There have been several excellent publications in recent years concerning the history of Grantham and I hope that this book can complement these and supply fresh information on topics of interest.

The informed reader will notice that there are several gaps in the content of the book which they may feel affects its continuity; this has been done deliberately as I see little point in repeating what has been fully covered in previous publications. The primary objective of the book, as far as I am concerned, is to share some part of my postcard, photograph and ephemera collection with as many interested people as possible. My hope is that they find the collection as fascinating and enjoyable as I have done over the past twenty or so years it has taken me to compile.

The majority of the reproductions contained in this book are from postcards and we have, for the most part, our Edwardian forebears to thank for this as the postcard, at this time, was one of the main means of communication. Enterprising photographers could find a ready market for images of local and national events. Their pictures were sometimes published with remarkable rapidity, perhaps only a day after the occasion took place.

Over the years the importance of these small pieces of card had largely been ignored and it is only since the 1970s that topographical postcard collecting has once again become a popular hobby and to some a passion. It was realized that the images which the postcards contained had often altered beyond recognition or had entirely disappeared. The messages on the reverse, boringly matter of fact when written, had in many instances become little gems of social history and without the comments on the back a great deal of uncaptioned postcards would never be identified.

Grantham is a typical example of the need to retain the photographic archive that has been produced by both local and national photographers as major alterations have taken place, especially in the fifties and sixties. Without their contribution there would be many more gaps in our knowledge and understanding of the town.

If a cross-section of Grantham people were asked what they thought had made the greatest contribution in the forming of the town as it is today answers would fall into several widely contrasting categories. Those with a knowledge of the town's more ancient history might suggest that the wealth brought to the town by the wool merchants of the thirteenth century would have been a major influence in the earlier years. The Grey Friars ingenuity in bringing fresh water to the population in the fourteenth century was an important contribution to the health and stability of the community.

The arrival of the engineering industry in the nineteenth century to what had previously been predominately an agricultural area was to have immense significance for the town and its population. This I am sure most people would agree with, but would this have happened without another major factor that shapes a town's destiny, that of transport. The Great North Road, now the A1 trunk road, ran through Grantham before the town was bypassed in the early 1960s. This brought the need for coaching inns so weary travellers had somewhere to stay during a journey that in the eighteenth and nineteenth centuries could take days, compared with a few hours today. The Grantham to Nottingham Canal was opened in the 1790s so that Grantham could transport produce and goods to and from the Trent area. In the early 1850s the town had its first railway line to the outskirts of Nottingham and within a few years the Great Northern Railway had put Grantham on its main east coast line.

The two world wars would be the choice of some as the influence that shaped the town. During the First World War the two large army training camps at Belton and Harrowby were to have an immediate effect on the area in and around the town. In the Second World War the town was a regular target for the *Luftwaffe* because of all the industry now providing weapons for the war effort. They were also interested in Grantham's railway, which had a busy loco area that included engine sheds and a goods yard.

In recent times it could be said that the coming of the supermarkets have had a profound effect. They have replaced whole streets and communities in the town centre and have also been instrumental in moving interest from the once well-established shopping areas. This is not a criticism as it is the way of the world we live in today, but it is certainly a contributing factor of how we see the town as we move into a new century.

To try and decide what has had the most influence on our community would be purely a personal preference. The truth of the matter is that every one of them and many others not mentioned here have each had their part to play in shaping the town that we live in today. Most have passed into history and all we have left as proof of their existence are the memories of the older generations and the artefacts, ephemera and photographs that have survived through the years. I have tried to save as much of this as I can and am pleased to share a part of my collection with you in this book, hoping it gives as much pleasure to read as it did to write.

Fred Leadbetter
January 2000

Bibliography

White's Directories of Lincolnshire, various dates
Kelly's Directories of Lincolnshire, various dates
Palmer's Almanacs, various dates
Harrison's Almanacs, various dates
Grantham *Red Books*, various dates
Grantham Journal
Bygone Grantham, by Malcolm Knapp and Michael Pointer
A History of the Kings School, Grantham, by S.J. Branson BSc, 1988

One
The Southern
Approach to Grantham

The Fox Inn. South Witham.

We start our journey into Grantham, like thousands before us, on the Great North Road. The Fox Inn is situated on this main thoroughfare, close to the Rutland and Lincolnshire border, with South Witham in the river valley to the west. Since this view was taken in the 1930s, the inn has been extended to include the row of small cottages on its northern end.

This old tower mill stood on the outskirts of the village of South Witham for over 100 years before coming to the end of its working life in the 1920s, helped on its way by a lightning strike in that decade. Two millstones and a date plate of 1793 still exist on the property next to the field where this once elegant building stood. These artefacts and a grassy mound are all that is left to remind us of its existence.

A few miles south of North Witham the river from which it takes its name begins its winding journey to Boston and the sea beyond. The footbridge on the right in this view of the village from around 1900 straddles the young watercourse, which at this stage is little more than a stream.

This is the children's festival parade through Colsterworth in 1906. The parade took place in May each year and ended with a maypole dance in one of the nearby fields. Many villages had similar parades, but it is remarkable to note that this one in Colsterworth is marching down the Great North Road, the A1 trunk road of today.

The children of Colsterworth making a good job of decorating the maypole, again in 1906.

Post Lane in Colsterworth can no longer boast a single dwelling along its narrow way, but in the early 1900s these small cottages graced its edges.

By far the most famous son of Woolsthorpe by Colsterworth is Sir Isaac Newton, the great scientist and mathematician, but over the years of the hamlet's existence it has been the ordinary working man that has kept the community alive. Josiah Senescall was such a man and he is seen here on the left of the picture with his foot resting on one of his beloved ploughing engines. Josiah, nicknamed 'Sergeant' after a career in the royal artillery, ran a pair of these machines which he called Jack and Jill. He also served the local populace as a rabbit catcher and a chimney sweep. His young daughter Rene is seen here on the footplate in this late 1920s scene.

The Queen public house was on the northern outskirts of Colsterworth on the corner of Woolsthorpe Road and Bridge End. When this photograph was taken in the early 1900s the publican was Albert Vale. Although closed in 1913 the building is still going strong as a private house.

A view of South Gate Lodge, Easton Park, c. 1910. The lodge was demolished in the 1960s, but the gates and pillars almost saw out the century, failing only by weeks when they were removed in late 1999. As demonstrated by the lady with the pram on the left, in the early years of the century one could still take a leisurely stroll down the Great North Road.

By the early 1800s the Cholmeleys had rebuilt much of Easton Hall in the Elizabethan style and when this postcard was sent in 1915 the Hall was a very grand building. This scene shows the extension on the left of the Hall that was built in 1911. During the Second World War it was the home of the royal artillery and then the parachute regiment. It was to survive for only a few years after the hostilities, being demolished in 1950.

The entrance gate to Easton Hall was built in 1841 and is all that now remains of what must have been a truly splendid country house.

The post office at Stoke Rochford was demolished in the late 1950s when it became a casualty of the A1 road-widening scheme. This view, dating from around 1913, shows the family of the sub-postmaster John Parker posing for the camera.

South Lodge, at the entrance gates to Stoke Rochford park, was built in the 1830s and since this scene was captured on camera around 1910, a wall and embankment have been added, eliminating the pillar and railings on the far right.

The present Stoke Rochford Hall, like Easton Hall across the Great North Road, was also built in the Elizabethan style. Between 1840 and 1845 the Turner family built this fine example of early Victorian architecture. After the Second World War it was used as a teacher training college and in 1977 was bought by the National Union of Teachers. It is now a conference and leisure centre.

This is how it was for the privileged motorist in the early 1930s. Comfy cane chairs and waiter service, a far cry from the plastic furniture and fast food of today. Some of the first seats in the Stoke Rochford Roadhouse were old pews that had been replaced in nearby Stoke and Easton church. The Roadhouse was situated close by the entrance to Stoke Rochford golf course before it suffered a major fire in 1960 and closed in 1963.

There has been a Blue Horse pub on the Great North Road at Great Ponton since the first half of the nineteenth century. This view from a postcard that was used in 1944 shows James Hole's brewery lorry making a delivery of ale for the publican, Mr Albert Barter's clientele.

The Edwardians could certainly put on a good parade and the population of Great Ponton were no exception. When the Amicable Society marched through the village in 1910 everyone turned out in their Sunday best to watch or take part in the procession.

The Grantham Waterworks Company was formed in the early 1850s. This postcard from around 1925 shows their water treatment works at Saltersford in the Witham valley and gives a good view of the original steam pumping station that operated until 1936, after which oil engines were introduced.

Originally referred to as the fever tents by the locals, the isolation hospital on Gorse Lane was opened in 1896. By the time this postcard was sent in 1906 it had been transformed into these more permanent buildings. The postcard was sent by the little boy standing first left to his friend Freddy, saying that he is now well and looking forward to coming home.

Two

Spittlegate and New Somerby

WHALEBONE LANE NEAR GRANTHAM.

Nothing now remains of these whale jaw-bones, which spanned the lane joining Somerby Hill to Little Ponton, and gave it its name. When erected by the Victorians the whale bones stood eighteen feet at their highest point but over the years they suffered the ravages of time and the local children's eagerness for a small piece as a keepsake.

The carrier's van accident on Somerby Hill on 25 May 1907 – in which three people were killed and several injured – stands as an example of how swiftly the postcard photographers of the day reached an incident. Walter Wheeler took this photograph and had it and others like it for sale within days of the tragic occurrence.

Even the unfortunate carrier, Mr J.W. Wilkinson of Lenton, was seen as a good bet to sell a postcard or two and Wheeler duly obliged, recording his image for later generations of local historians. Mr Wilkinson, who did his best to stop his horse from bolting, was found to be blameless at the subsequent inquest and a verdict of accidental death was the decision reached by the jury.

The winter of 1947 saw heavy snow throughout the country. Here, the local firm of F. Swallow & Son are busy loading forage into an aircraft at Spittlegate aerodrome to feed livestock on hard-pressed Welsh farms.

In 1922 Grantham had one of its worst floods in living memory. One of the casualties was the bridge in Witham Place which was washed away by the torrent. The next major floods occurred in 1932 and in an attempt to save the bridge from being lost a second time an Aveling & Porter steamroller belonging to the council was attached to the structure by steel cables. In the event the flood was not as destructive as anticipated and the precautions were not required. This view looks down into Witham Place with Bridge End Road at the bottom and Bridge Street on the left.

On 14 June 1906 the Bishop of Lincoln came to Grantham to lay the foundation stone of Saint Anne's church on Harrowby Road, New Somerby. He is seen here reading the dedication.

THE BISHOP OF LINCOLN LAYING THE
FOUNDATION STONE OF ST ANNE'S CHURCH, NEW SOMERBY, GRANTHAM.

The new church replaced the original, which was built around 1884, and was situated close by between Harrowby Road and Cecil Street. This was affectionately referred to as the tin tabernacle because it was constructed from iron sheeting. Judging by the large crowd in this scene, the church had a good congregation for its first ceremony.

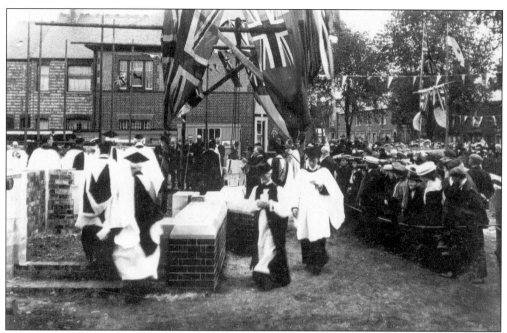

The bishop and his clergy move among the scaffolding and bricks as the foundation stone is lowered into place. By the time the building was finished the cost was between £3,000 and £4,000.

On 30 May 1907 the Bishop of Lincoln returned to Grantham to dedicate the church and the photographer was on hand once more to record the occasion. Within two years of the official opening an appeal was launched to raise a further £1,000 to pay off all remaining debts and build a vicarage.

NEW SOMERBY, GRANTHAM.

WANTED, A MILE OF PENNIES

To clear off the debt on St. Anne's Church, New Somerby, Grantham. Will you be so good as to help and interest others? 30 Pennies make 1 Yard.

REV. G. G. WALKER,
SOMERBY RECTORY,
GRANTHAM.

MISS J. E. SNEATH,
17, St. CATHERINE'S ROAD,
GRANTHAM.

This postcard was part of one idea that was used as a fundraising exercise to help collect the money required. The recipient of the postcard was encouraged to assist in the collection of a mile of pennies. The postcard states that 30 pennies make a yard and as there were 240 old pennies to the pound it was hoped that this particular effort would raise £220.

The interior of the church in 1933 showing the decorations for the harvest festival. The Parish Rooms of the old church still exist today behind Nos 49 to 52 Cecil Street, although the iron roof has long gone. Nothing remains of the old church, however, which was situated between King Edward's Terrace and Newton Terrace on Harrowby Road.

The Revd G.G. Walker was the first rector of the new church, but St Anne's and its congregation can be traced back to the 1870s. Here are some important dates in its history:

January 1875: Cottage service.
September 1875: Services in the Cemetery Chapel on Sundays and Fridays.
November 1878: Services in the newly opened Church School, which was used as a day school and as Mission church.
January 1884: Services in the Iron Church.
May 1907: Services in the new church.

The Revd Edwin Millard was Vicar-designate when this photograph was taken in 1908, but one year later he was to take Revd Walker's place. He remained in the post until 1950, retiring then only because of ill-health.

South Parade in the early 1920s. The houses on the extreme right are on the corner of Albert Street and were badly damaged by bombs in the Second World War. The site remained vacant for many years but has recently been redeveloped into more housing.

Dickinson's shop was located near the South Parade end of Albert Street, close to Albert Terrace. This postcard shows Miss Dickinson in the doorway of the shop in 1907. The little independent corner shop has now mainly passed into history, overwhelmed by the march of time, but when this photograph was taken nearly every street had at least one shop; often just an ordinary house with the front room converted into business premises.

The original name of Houghton Road was Paper Mill Lane as there had been a mill at the end of this road for at least 150 years. The first recorded owners were James and Suzannah Courtley in 1742 and from 1838 to 1872 it was run by the Hornsby family. This view shows the road in the late 1920s almost three decades after the Earl of Dysart sold the land adjacent to the recreation ground, which also included the land on the south side of Bridge End Road. This resulted in the building of houses that subsequently enclosed the leisure area.

Bandstand Dysart Park Grantham.

In 1922 the unemployed men of Grantham were set to work on a project that saw the recreation grounds transformed into what is known today as Dysart Park. The official opening took place on 28 July 1927 but many of the facilities, including the bandstand shown here, were in use before this date.

A view looking towards Bridge End Road from Dysart Park bandstand in 1937.

The paddling pool in Dysart Park was a very popular place for the children of Grantham, as this 1933 postcard demonstrates. It was situated in the south-eastern corner of the park, close to the River Witham with the outdoor swimming baths next door.

The Co-op had been established in Grantham since 1872, with its main buildings being situated on the corner of Saint Catherine's Road and Saint Peter's Hill. The company quickly expanded to other areas of the town and this Bridge End Road shop, officially No. 4 branch, has a date of 1911 on one of its rainwater heads. The site, originally occupied by a farm and its orchard, eventually included the company's dairy, slaughterhouse and bakery in Inner Street.

A view of the Wesleyan chapel on Bridge End Road in the 1890s. The Assembly Rooms and Sunday school, which are now a nightclub, were built later, in the early 1900s. The congregation are assembled outside for the annual Sunday school outing. At this time the Sunday school was in rooms built in 1879 at the rear of the building. The chapel was erected in 1875 on ground donated by William Hornsby. It closed its doors for the last time at Christmas 1964 and was demolished soon after.

The interior of the chapel on the occasion of the Sunday school anniversary in 1935. Every year benches were erected round the pulpit and the children would all perform their party piece: it might be reciting a well-rehearsed poem or singing to the audience – either solo or, less dauntingly, in a group.

These ladies and gentlemen are the staff of the Sunday school at Bridge End Road's chapel around the time of the First World War. There are a total of twenty-two, confirming what a thriving family congregation there was at this time. Back row, left to right: Mr Joseph Kettle, Mr L. Broxholme, Mr Edmond Booth, -?-, Mr Jim Kettle, Mr George Armitage, Mr Archie Henson, -?-. Middle row: Miss Charles, Mrs Bowler, Mrs Wells, -?-, Mrs Kettle, Mrs Roberts, Miss Cook, Miss Parker. Front row: Miss Lassie, Mrs Dale, Mrs Street, Mrs Robinson, Mrs Armitage, Mrs Watchorn.

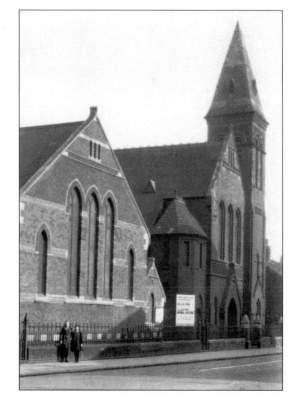

A view of the chapel in the 1930s showing it complete with its Assembly Rooms and Sunday school. The iron railings adorning its walls soon disappeared, like many others in the town, to feed the munitions factories in the Second World War.

When this photograph of Inner Street was taken in 1936 there was still a sizeable community living in the area. The building at the top of the street was Ruston & Hornsby's steam hammer shop, which was built in 1860 and was still one of the noisiest places in the factory complex. As well as the houses on the left of the scene there were many courts and yards around the corner on the right. These included Union Court, Bourne Cottages, Portland Place and Seaman's Yard. A good proportion of the housing's menfolk would have earned their living from the nearby factory, so they were not in a position to complain about the din. Although they had been part of the community since Victorian times, few of these courts and yards were to see out the 1930s. The building on the right was the Co-op bakery that opened in September 1911.

Pipe laying in the entrance to what was then and still is the gateway to the Inner Street allotments. There is often a crowd to watch men at work and this scene in the 1930s is no exception. The three ladies looking over the wall from their backyard lived in what was called Langstons Buildings.

Like many public houses, the Spotted Cow on London Road started life as a beer house but received its full licence when the Artichokes Inn in Swinegate was closed in 1921: the latter's licence was transferred to the former. This advertising postcard dates from around this time, when the publican was Mr S.A. Gante and the brewery was Warwicks & Richardsons.

Although much has already been written about Hornsby's engineering works, it would be wrong to pass along London Road without mentioning the business that has had such an influence on the town. Therefore, this image and the following three are included to show the company around the turn of the twentieth century. The group of oil engine fitters and erectors surround a Hornsby-Akroyd oil engine which was patented in 1890.

This is Hornsby's tracked vehicle in the early 1900s. It was this company that first developed the caterpillar track, which was used by British tanks with devastating effect a few years later in the First World War. On this occasion the test vehicle was on its way to what was then the recreation grounds along Bridge End Road for trials when it decided to take a sharp left and call in at one of the shops at the junction of London Road and Bridge End Road. Clearly more work was required on the steering mechanism.

An advertising postcard from a series produced for Hornsby's in the early 1900s, showing various types of machinery manufactured by the company.

In the First World War Hornsby's were busy manufacturing munitions and in 1916 these ladies – and one small boy – formed the workforce of the auto division in 15A shop. The site where this photograph was taken on London Road is now a garage forecourt.

Hornsby's were not the only engineering company to emerge in Spittlegate during the nineteenth century. The man in the photograph was James Coultas, who started making agricultural machinery in the 1850s and called his factory on Station road, opposite the railway station, 'The Perseverance Iron Works'. The company, which specialized in seed drills won many medals for its equipment and remained in business until 1956, supplying the farming industry all over the world for more than 100 years.

A view of Coultas' yard in the 1890s. The railway station can be seen on the left of this photograph.

An interior view of Coultas' factory showing a busy and untidy machine shop around the same date.

A south-facing view of Coultas' yard, also in the last decade of the nineteenth century.

On the corner of Railway Terrace and Grantley Street was a long-established public house called the Layton Arms. This view from around 1900 shows the premises when the publican was a Mr Mathew Dack. The street bollards are a nice touch – if anyone was to exit the premises after imbibing perhaps a little to much liquid refreshment, at least they would not fall into the road under the wheels of a passing horse and cart.

The population of Railway Terrace turned out in force for this photograph taken in 1935. It shows another view of the Layton Arms public house, this time decorated for the town's centenary celebrations. It closed in 1956 and the door on the corner was bricked up. The premises reopened as the Junction Inn before closing for good in the early 1960s.

On the opposite corner of Grantley Street and Railway Terrace was Streeton's butchers shop. The remains of the shop can still be seen but the premises are in the process of alteration. The window would lift up to reveal the meat for sale laid out on a marble slab, until recently still in situ. Like the previous view, this postcard was produced by George Scothern for the centenary celebrations of 1935.

The London Road football and cricket ground is now the site of a supermarket and its car park, but for many years it was used by the people of Grantham for sport as well as an arena in which many occasions and festivities were celebrated. This is the culmination of the parade which took place in 1911 as part of the celebrations for the Coronation of George V when Lord and Lady Brownlow reviewed the participating organizations, in this instance the Grantham company of the Boys Brigade.

This is the same occasion with Lord Brownlow walking the lines of a contingent of the Grantham Boy Scouts. The first Grantham group was formed in 1909, with the scoutmaster being the Revd A.M. Cook, a teacher at the Kings School.

This slightly earlier scene shows the finale of the 1906 May Day parade when the participants gathered on the sports ground to watch the local children dance around the maypole. The houses in the background are part of Harrow Street.

It should not be forgotten that the ground was first and foremost a sports field, hosting many charity events as well as professional fixtures. In 1913 this Grantham Borough Police football team played a charity match against the Grantham Fire Brigade eleven.

The Grantham Rovers football club was in its heyday in the 1890s, but these players from two decades later were still willing to put on the old strip when duty called. They had been enticed out of retirement to play a charity match against the Comrades of the Great War for the benefit of the Comrades War Association and the Lincolnshire Prisoners of War Fund. Although reported as a slow game, the Rovers' ball skills predominated and gave them a 2-1 victory. The Rovers team were; back row, from left to right: Brittain, Ellis, Beck. Middle row: Halliday, Slater, Chamberlain (captain). Front row: Turner, Bennett, John Senior, Allen, James Senior.

When this Grantham football club team were playing in 1916 the town's coat of arms was proudly displayed on the players' shirts.

An early Grantham town programme from 1914 when the local team played Derby reserves. As can be seen from the crossed out name, there must have been a late team change after going to press.

GRANTHAM FOOTBALL CLUB.

Grand Central Alliance Match.

Grantham v. Derby County Reserves.

LONDON ROAD GROUND,

Saturday, 21st February, 1914.

SELECTED TEAMS:—

Right.		DERBY.		Left.
		Lawrence.		
	Cullen.		Skelton.	
	Leney.	Hall.	Bagshaw.	
Reader.	Methven.	Bloomer.	Henderson.	Neve.

v.

Left.		GRANTHAM.		Right.
Howard.	Eatch	Tonge.	Marriott.	Woodruff. Duckett
	Clay.	Bavin.	Henshaw.	
	Bettison.		Smith.	
		Humphreys.		

KICK-OFF 3-30 P.M.

PALMER & SON, GRANTHAM.

GRANTHAM FOOTBALL CLUB.

Balance Sheet, Season 1913-14.

REVENUE ACCOUNT.

SEASON 1912-13. £ s. d.	INCOME.	£ s. d.	SEASON 1912-13. £ s. d.	EXPENDITURE.	£ s. d.
16 12 3	Balance ...	9 9 7	253 19 0	Players' Wages and Lost Time ...	223 14 6
355 16 4½	Gate Receipts ...	366 12 8	20 2 6	Trainers' Wages and Washing ...	17 1 2
15 18 10½	Half Share of Gates from other Clubs	6 4 0	132 12 11	Railway Fares and Teas ...	105 10 7
32 1 3	Subscriptions, &c. ...	80 7 9	35 2 0½	Half Share of Gates ...	39 0 6
114 14 4	Sports, &c. ...	130 17 3	79 13 10½	Sports, &c. ...	91 12 1
133 10 0	Transfer Fees ...	20 0 0	18 9 0	Grand Stand ...	12 16 5
9 6	Boston Town Non-fulfilment of Fixture	Nil.	20 8 2½	Training Room and Ground Expenses	18 2 8
1 6 8	Guarantee from Club ...	1 5 8	14 13 11	Guarantees to Clubs ...	8 0 0
1 1 11	Telegram Money Returned ...	16 8	19 2 2	Referees ...	15 10 8
Nil.	Supporters' Club for Stand Roof ...	12 0 0	7 16 0	New Boiler ...	Nil.
Nil.	Gift—Supporters' Club ...	5 0 0	20 2 6	Rent of Ground ...	20 0 0
Nil.	Adverts. ...	10 0	16 16 11½	Printing, Advertising and Stationery	17 0 7
10 3	Sub-Letting Stand ...	5 3 8	4 18 0	Posting Bills ...	3 11 0
			3 7 4	10% Cup Ties Lincs. F.A. ...	3 14 1
			6 10 4	Police ...	5 11 7
			5 18 1	Postages, Telegrams, Registered Letters, Carriage, &c. ...	5 14 7
			1 4 7	Registration, Professional and Transfer Forms ...	1 16 10
			5 7 0	Entries & Subs. to League & Cups....	4 13 6
			6 18 10	Boots, Knickers and Footballs ...	6 14 11
			2 0 0	Transfer Fees ...	2 10 0
			Nil.	Doctors' Bills ...	3 11 6
			6 10 4	Insurance of Players ...	6 1 6
			1 10 0	Bank Charges ...	2 1 4
			17 10	Sundries ...	16 7½
			6 0 0	Transfer to Capital Account for Stand	5 0 0
			9 9 7	Balance ...	18 1 1¼
£692 1 5		£638 7 3	£692 1 5		£638 7 3

CAPITAL ACCOUNT.

	INCOME.	£ s. d.		EXPENDITURE.	£ s. d.
Revenue Account		5 0 0	Balance brought forward		5 0 0

BALANCE SHEET.

	LIABILITIES.	£ s. d.		ASSETS.	£ s. d.
Sundry Creditors		29 0 0	Stand and other effects		40 9 0
Surplus		30 10 6	Sundry Debtors		1 0 4
			Revenue Account Balance		18 1 1¼
		£59 10 6			£59 10 6

JOHN C. WHETSTONE, Hon. Sec.
JOHN WELBORN, Hon. Treasurer.

Audited and found correct, 23rd June, 1914.

(Signed) E. L. DAVIES.
(Signed) G. STEVENSON.

Palmer & Son, Grantham.

A balance sheet of the town's football club for the 1913-14 season which has several interesting items listed. For instance, a supporters club was already active, giving a gift of £5 and a further £12 towards the stand roof, and a sum of £20 came into the coffers in transfer fees, equalling the amount paid out for the year's ground rent.

A view of London Road dating from the early years of the First World War. The sender of the postcard complains that the hotel he is staying at is full of army officers and all he could get was a single bed. Obviously some of the senior ranks preferred the comforts of Grantham's hostelries to what was on offer at Belton and Harrowby army camps.

George Burrell opened his general drapers shop in Grantham in 1885 but when this photograph was taken in the early 1890s he had also become a milliner. Here, his staff are gathered outside the shop, this time numbered 20 and 21 London Road. The premises are now occupied by a company selling disability aids. Notice the superb gas light in the shop doorway.

Three
Saint Peter's Hill and Wharf Road

'God bless our King and Queen' proclaim the banners in a view of Saint Peter's Hill showing the decorations for the Coronation of George VI in 1937. The sunshade at 1 London Road, on the right of the picture, informs us that these are the premises of Walter Lee's photographic shop and studio.

There are many postcards featuring Saint Peter's Hill but this one facing south is one of the more unusual views. It shows the fine row of town houses on the right that were replaced by the first post office on this site in the early 1920s.

A general view of Saint Peter's Hill showing very little traffic other than the lone cyclist who seems disinclined to ride near the side of the road. This leisurely scene from the early 1900s gives an impression that life was lived at a slower pace in these first years of the twentieth century.

This branch of the Star Supply Stores was situated at 37 Saint Peter's Hill, occupying the frontage that was previously the coachbuilding works of Richard Anderson. The photograph dates from the early 1920s and, as can be seen from the window dressing, it must have been close to Christmas. The Star Supply Stores were formerly called the Star Tea Company and this shop was one of two in the town, the other being in narrow Westgate. Both shops did business in the town for many years, eventually finishing with the more well-known name of the International Stores.

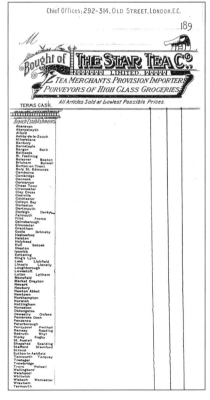

Chief Offices; 292-314. Old Street, London, E.C.

189

Bought of **THE STAR TEA Cº** LIMITED.

TEA MERCHANTS, PROVISION IMPORTERS PURVEYORS OF HIGH CLASS GROCERIES

All Articles Sold at Lowest Possible Prices.

TERMS CASH.

Branch Establishments
Aberavon
Aberystwyth
Alford
Ashby-de-la-Zouch
Atherstone
Banbury
Barnstaple
Bangor   Bath
Bethesda
Bl. Festiniog
Bolsover   Boston
Brixham   Bulwell
Burton-on-Trent
Bury St. Edmunds
Camborne
Cambridge
Cannock
Carnarvon
Chase Town
Cirencester
Clay Cross
Coalville
Colchester
Colwyn Bay
Darlaston
Dartmouth   Derby
Denbigh
Falmouth
Flint   Frome
Gainsborough
Gloucester
Grantham
Goole   Grimsby
Hednesford
Helston
Holyhead
Hull   Ibstock
Ilkeston
Ipswich
Kettering
King's Lynn
Leek   Lichfield
Lincoln   Llanelly
Loughborough
Lowestoft
Luton   Lytham
Mansfield
Market Drayton
Newark
Newbury
Newton Abbot
Newtown
Northampton
Norwich
Nottingham
Nuneaton
Oakengates
Oswestry   Oxford
Pembroke Dock
Penzance
Peterborough
Pontypool   Pwllheli
Ramsey   Reading
Redruth   Rhyl
Ripley   Rugby
St. Austell
Shepshed   Spalding
Stafford   Stamford
Stroud
Sutton-in-Ashfield
Tamworth   Torquay
Tredegar
Trowbridge
Truro   Walsall
Wallingboro'
Walshpool
Whitwick
Wisbech   Worcester
Wrexham
Yarmouth

This billhead for the Star Tea Company from the 1890s shows how widespread the business was before changing its name to the Star Supply Stores. There are approximately 100 town names on the left and some, like Grantham, had more than one store trading at the same time.

The building on the right of this photograph, taken from Birdcage Walk, was built in the late eighteenth century as a private house. However, this view dating from around 1905 shows it as the Fernside School for Young Ladies, when it was run by Miss Margaret Hancock. The school closed in 1917 and the premises became a soup kitchen for a time, eventually being taken over by John Hall's furnishing business which moved from the Market Place in the early 1920s. It is now the home of the Lloyds-TSB bank.

Grantham's original Guildhall was situated at the top of Guildhall Street. It was demolished and the present Guildhall was built on Saint Peter's Hill in the late 1860s. The fine Victorian building is shown here amid decorations for the Coronation of George V in 1911.

Another view of the Guildhall, this time in 1915. The old houses just in view on the right were eventually replaced by the Grantham Library and Museum building, which opened in 1926.

In the early 1900s Whipple's garage was the local agent for the Argyll company and here staff are seen outside the Guildhall with one of their models. All are suitably attired for whatever the weather may have in store for them.

In 1906 the Skegness lifeboat was brought to town for a publicity and fundraising exercise. It was transported from Skegness by rail and was pulled round the town by a team of horses provided by the Belton park estate. The lifeboat is shown outside the Guildhall just before beginning its journey to the canal basin up Old Wharf Road, where it was to be launched.

The town fire brigade took part in the lifeboat parade and can be seen proudly showing off what was, in 1906, their state-of-the-art fire-fighting equipment. When this photograph was taken the fire engine was housed in the Guildhall complex and the horses were stabled to the rear.

The lifeboat parade sets off down Birdcage walk. This postcard was sent to a young lady in Somerset by her Aunt Nell who states that she is in the photograph and can her niece find her in the crowd?

The highlight of the day was the launch of the lifeboat in the canal basin up Old Wharf Road and judging by the assembled crowd this was an occasion not to be missed.

Now here is a fine body of men! This is a float from the Mayday parade of 1906 and shows a group of the Grantham Boys Brigade posing for the camera behind the Guildhall. The brigade was formed more than 100 years ago and although no longer active in Grantham, is still very much alive in other areas of the country. The Grantham Brigade's uniforms, rifles and regalia were stored in an upstairs room of the Wesleyan chapel on Bridge End Road and may well have been lost prior to the chapel's demise in the 1960s. The cart belonged to a Grantham carrier called George T. Cook who lived and worked from Fletcher Cottage, otherwise known as 5 Fletcher Street, on the corner of Norton Street.

A view from Wharf Road looking up Commercial Road into Spittlegate. The decorations were for George V's silver jubilee in 1935, showing a scene little changed over the years. The Victoria Hotel on the corner of William Street closed its doors for the last time in 1977. Johnson's butchers shop on the corner of Wharf Road is now a gentlemen's hairdressers.

A postcard showing the Grantham fire brigade pumping water out of C.W. Dixon's cellars after the floods in 1932. Dixon began trading at this shop on Wharf Road as a cabinetmaker in the latter half of the nineteenth century and by the 1930s he had become a general furniture dealer and warehouseman.

This view of Dixons is on a happier occasion, showing the decorations for the centenary of the Corporation of Grantham celebrations in 1935. The shop became Wallworks in the 1970s before disappearing to make way for the new bus station.

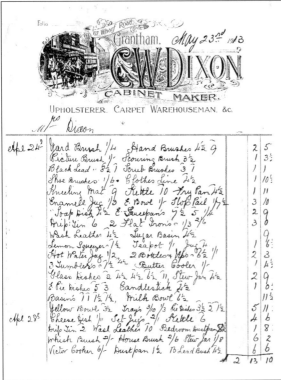

This billhead for C.W. Dixon was issued in 1913 and gives a feel for the cost of everyday items in that era. Remember that there were twelve old pennies to the shilling and a shilling is now equal to five new pence.

54

Spencer's cycle depot was on the corner of Norton Street and Wharf Road. Previously it had been the grocer's shop of Joseph King but when this postcard was sent in 1909 Spencer had been in residence for several years and was to remain there into the 1920s. Many locals will remember the premises as Grantham's army recruiting offices.

This 1950s postcard shows the southern end of Welby Street with the Durham Ox public house in its last years of business: it was to close in the early 1960s. The scene also shows a view of Cheshire's chemist shop whose business had been in Wharf Road since the 1840s.

Rutland Street in 1935, just one of the communities that disappeared in the redevelopment along Wharf Road in the late 1970s and early 1980s. These houses were on what is now Morrison's car park.

Four

Dysart Road and the Harlaxton Road Area

Road works at the bottom of Dysart Road in 1936. The row of buildings beyond the workmen have now all disappeared and Sankt Augustin Way bisects the road just before the main-line railway bridge.

Potter's factory on Dysart Road could not be said to hide its light under a bushel – as this postcard of 1922 shows, they certainly knew how to advertise. The firm manufactured various types of pumping machinery and remained in business until the 1930s, after which the premises were taken over by the crane makers, R.H. Neale. The site is now the home of Autumn Park trading estate.

Council workmen were laying a footpath on Dysart Road in this 1930s scene and over on the left the photographer has caught a glimpse of what was Grantham's third and last workhouse. Most of the people who remember the buildings would have known them as Hill View hospital, the majority of which was demolished in the late 1960s.

THE CANAL
GRANTHAM.

W.R.C.WHEELER.
GRANTHAM.

At the turn of the twentieth century this bridge over the Grantham to Nottingham Canal was called Hollis' bridge and was situated on what at that time was called Hollis' Lane. Its official title was bridge No. 69 but in later years the road's name was changed to Earlsfield Lane and because of the bridge's proximity to Shaw's Tannery it was named Skinyard Bridge by the locals. In 1957 the Grantham end of the canal was filled in and the waterway now ends on the site where this bridge once stood.

Although the Grantham canal did not officially close until 1936, by the time this photograph was taken around 1905 much of its trade had been lost to the railways. However as can be clearly seen, the swing bridge was still in good working order. The bridge is now long gone but still lives on in name as the link road between Harlaxton Road and Trent Road is called Swingbridge Road.

This view of Harlaxton Road in the 1930s shows a motorcar just turning out of Springfield Road, a junction that was to move some yards towards the town in later years. The major housebuilding programme in this area is still to come and the few houses that can be seen behind the car are in Belvoir Avenue. George Neale had these dwellings built on land he bought in 1903; the last block was finished in 1910. George had taken over the house furnishing business of Hannett, Kellam and New in Atlas House, Westgate, and these houses were for his managers and workmen. He was later to live in Anstey Lodge, which is just to the left of the telegraph pole and is now 299 Harlaxton Road.

Another 1930s view from the same place in Harlaxton Road as the last picture, this time looking towards Grantham and showing the mass of allotments that had been established in this area for many years. The houses in the background are on Huntingtower Road and on the skyline can be seen the new coaling tower for the railway engine sheds. This remained a Grantham landmark until it was demolished in the 1960s.

A much earlier scene on Harlaxton Road and one closer to the town centre. There are no houses between Huntingtower Road and the railway bridge as most of these were not built until the 1920s. This postcard was sent in 1915 when the lady riding her bike down the centre of the road felt quite safe in doing so.

The Huntingtower Arms, situated on the corner of Huntingtower Road and Harlaxton Road, was the only public house in Grantham to receive a licence during the First World War. This view shows the premises in the early 1920s when the publican was Frederick B. Pickworth.

There is a state-of-the-art self-service filling station on this site on Harlaxton Road today but in 1963 the haulage firm of Jack Harris would give you the personal touch with this solitary pump. The row of buildings festooned with billboard posters were Jack's warehouses and garages.

Another view of Jack Harris' garages taken at the same time as the previous photograph. Harry Worth was in his heyday in the 1960s and the poster on the right proclaims his star billing in *Turn again Wittington* at the Theatre Royal, Nottingham.

This scene is behind the buildings shown in the previous two views and shows Jack Harris' transport fleet in 1964.

In the 1930s Jack's firm was busy transporting goods for many local companies. Here is the man himself with one of James Coultas' seed drills in the railway yards next to the granary. Launder Terrace can be seen in the background.

When the Huntingtower Road ARP wardens were first formed their headquarters were in the offices of the Lincolnshire Road Car building that can be seen in the background. However, by the time this photograph was taken in 1943 they had moved to a purpose-built structure in the Springfield Arms public house backyard. The following people are included in the picture, although not all those present have been identified. Back row: H. Marvin, Mr Graik, Jack Putman, C. Grimwood, B. Gowler. Second row: Edward Clipston, Mr Carpenter, Mr Wady, Mr Watson, W. Hill, Mr Hawkins, Mr Brown, Mr Ledger, Mr Bromley. Third row: H. Whitaker, Doris Rollings, Mrs Grimwood, Mr Wilde, Mr Stubley, Mr G. Mitcham, Mrs Watson, F. Flood. Front row: G. Addison, H. Mitcham, B. Hill. George Mitcham, sixth from the left on the third row was a Grantham schoolteacher for many years and was also a local historian of some standing.

Five

Westgate and the Market Place

A north-facing view of wide Westgate in the 1950s, probably taken early in the morning before this normally busy thoroughfare came to life.

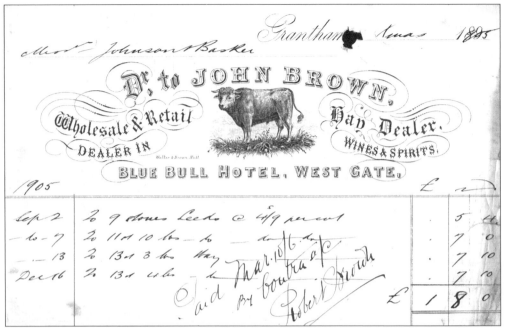

In 1905 John Brown ran the Blue Bull Hotel on the corner of Dysart Road and Westgate. He issued this bill over the Christmas period and may well have sent a reminder to follow as it was March 1906 before it was settled.

C. Basker & Sons were one of several pawnbrokers and jewellers in Grantham at the beginning of the twentieth century and their shop at 75 and 76 Westgate was almost opposite Welby Street.

The wine and spirit merchants Johnson, Basker and Co. were at 24 Westgate on the corner of Welby Street. Johnson started the business in the 1830s and was joined by Basker in the last quarter of the century. For a short time around 1890 they were also joined by Frederick Fletcher but he was soon to set up on his own elsewhere in Westgate. The building today is an amusement arcade and nightclub.

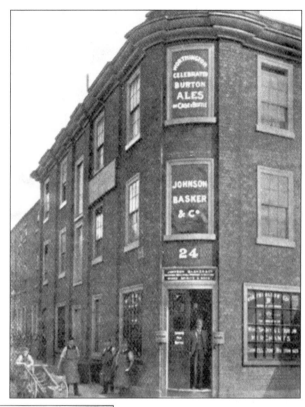

A billhead of Johnson, Basker & Co. dating from the 1890s. The prices shown would make any Channel day tripper's mouth water.

Complete Furnishing Warehouse, Atlas House, 77 and 78, Westgate, GRANTHAM,

June 13 188*7*

M*r Jas Hy Newcomt 37 [...]*

Bought of HANNETT, KELLAM & NEW

CABINET MAKERS, UPHOLSTERERS,
— PAPERHANGERS, —

Carpet Warehousemen, Glass and China Dealers, &c.

COFFINS MADE ON THE SHORTEST NOTICE.

FURNITURE REMOVERS TO ALL PARTS OF THE COUNTRY.

⁘ FURNITURE BOUGHT, SOLD OR EXCHANGED. ⁘

A billhead dated 1887 showing what sort of business Hannett, Kellam and New were running at Atlas House, Westgate. In this decade of the Victorian era they could completely furnish a house as well as being able to house the dead – and at very short notice. Hannett, in particular, was a very busy man in Grantham: he was mayor from 1882 to 1885 and in 1887 became an alderman. In the early 1880s, while being involved at Atlas House, he was also in partnership with Cammack at 12,13 and 14 Westgate.

This billhead of 1884 shows Hannett involved at both business premises in this year.

A view of the Malt Shovels public house in Westgate dating from the 1930s. It shows the publican Jack Buckley standing in the doorway with man's best friend by his side. As well as running the Malt Shovels, Jack played football for Grantham and was destined to sign for Doncaster Rovers. These premises are now a Chinese restaurant.

This 1920s view shows the archway in Guildhall Street that led to the back of the Blue Ram public house in Westgate. The entrance is still there although it has seen some alteration. The area beyond, however, has changed completely. The Blue Ram has reverted back to its original name of the King's Arms and there are now several thriving businesses within what is now called King's Walk.

A scene looking down into the Market Place from narrow Westgate, showing on the left the other Star Supply Store operating in Grantham in the first half of the century (see p. 47). The postcard dates from the early 1920s and shows how the horse was sharing the roads more and more with the motorcar.

Grantham Market Place has been at its present site since the fourteenth century, when it moved from in front of the parish church. This view dates from the early 1870s and shows a tranquil scene almost impossible to duplicate in the present day. On the left at No. 9 John Hall traded in glass and china, he also had No. 8 (just out of picture) where he was an undertaker, upholsterer and a purveyor of the pianoforte. No. 10 was the market cross vaults run by Garnett's wine and spirits merchants, which was next door to Broughton's London teahouse. Over the road, on the corner behind the cross was the town's general post office. It had been on this site at No. 19 Market Place since the middle of the 1800s.

The market cross was removed for the second time in 1884 as it was thought to be in a dangerous condition. It is also known that the cross was replaced by an obelisk in 1886. It is safe to assume that the top was removed immediately and the rest between these dates. Therefore, looking at the condition of the cross in this scene its date must fall somewhere between 1884 and 1886. The premises that were shown as Garnett's in the last picture have now become the Dysart Café, which was described in *White's Directory* as a coffee tavern. Broughton's were still selling tea next door and would continue to do so into the 1890s. The next four shops were replaced in 1891 by the buildings we see there today and the occupants were already making plans. The tall premises next to Broughton's was No. 12. The original site of the little dustpan, it was run by George Willoughby who had earlier opened his new hardware store at No. 2 Westgate, where the dustpan can still be seen over the shop window. No. 13 was the confectioner's shop of Edward Nickerson, who soon moved to No. 16, which was occupied at this time by the draper Richard Morley. Wand's butchers was at No. 14 and, although not very clear, the trade signs of a sheep and a cow can be seen over the shop window. The last of the four was the tobacconists and barbers shop of Henry Healey. The general post office was still at No. 19 until it moved in the early 1890s over the road to No. 9, previously the china shop of John Hall.

This picture is almost the same view as the previous one but forty years later in 1925. It shows the buildings that replaced the old block in 1891. The premises that were occupied by Broughton's tea house in the older picture were replaced in 1904 by the building that is still there today. In this scene it was the home of Piper's Penny Bazaar.

When this postcard was published in the first decade of the twentieth century Hepworths and Garratts were still in the Market Place, both eventually moved to the High Street. The obelisk which replaced the cross in the 1880s was soon to reach the end of its short life-span.

Before having their own premises purpose-built on the High Street in 1911, Chambers occupied several other locations close by. These included a brief spell in Whichcote House on Watergate, the shop on the corner of Butcher's Row and High Street and these buildings between the Royal Oak and the Chequers public houses. Chambers advertised themselves as the sole proprietor and manufacturer of the world famous Syston blanket, so named because they were made from the wool of the sheep from Syston Park.

Another scene from the early 1900s, clearly showing the cobbles that in some areas of the Market Place still exist under the present-day tarmac. The fine façade of Peark's stores split in two before the First World War and half became Ogden's seed stores, which it remained until the late 1980s. To the right of the conduit is the Blue Sheep Inn which was to close in 1915, a short time after this photograph was taken.

MARKET PLACE, GRANTHAM.

Charles Sharpe had traded in Grantham since the middle of the 1800s and this view of his premises on the corner of Westgate and the Market Place dates from around 1905. This postcard was produced to advertise his seed warehouse which not only catered for local needs but sold its produce to companies all over the world. Charles was a Sleaford man and the company's seed grounds were situated at Heckington and Great Hale. The shop closed in 1986 and is sadly missed by many green-fingered Granthamians.

Walter Plumb, the mayor in 1910, reads the proclamation of George V from the base of the obelisk. Hall's upholsterers and cabinetmakers, seen here behind the column, left the Market Place in the early 1920s to take up residence on Saint Peter's Hill in the building previously occupied by the Fernside School for Young Ladies. The post office moved across the Market Place in the 1890s from No. 19 to the premises next to Halls and can be seen on the right of this view. It remained on this site until it too relocated to Saint Peter's Hill, moving to purpose-built facilities in 1922.

This role of honour hung in the post office in the Market Place for the duration of the First World War. As can be seen, the right-hand date for the end of the war is still not known. It was not only to honour the dead but also to name the staff that had answered their country's call in its time of need. The names with an asterisk alongside were those of soldiers that had lost their lives in the conflict. The war memorial in the present post office tells us that ten of the men named on this roll of honour were never to return home after the war.

It is January 1911 and Lord Brownlow, who was mayor at the time, is seen officiating at the ceremony celebrating the return of the cross to the Market Place. The cross had lain in George Priest's builders yard in Wharf Road for more than twenty-five years before being returned to this site, its rightful resting place.

Six

High Street and Watergate

The Lloyds Bank building on the right of this view was erected in 1921 and this scene shows it prominently placed at the southernmost end of the High Street in the mid-1920s. The Bank sign no longer exists over the entrance but years of English weather has etched its shape into the local Ancaster stone. The gentleman on the bicycle is about to pass the Horse and Jockey public house, whose main doorway was not on the main thoroughfare, but situated in the entrance that led to the Horse and Jockey Yard, behind the building from which it took its name.

At the turn of the century the High Street consisted of several fine old buildings and this postcard serves as one way to record their existence now that many of them are no longer with us. Two of Grantham's old hotels feature in this scene of 1910. The street lamp on the left stands outside the White Hart and across the road to the right of the horse and cart is the archway of the Red Lion.

A comparable setting, but this time the High Street is decorated for the Coronation of George V a year later. To the right of the Red Lion Hotel the premises of Campion's cycle stores can be seen. They later moved to premises on the north side of the hotel before leaving the High Street altogether to spend a considerable time in Guildhall Street, moving with the times to become motor engineers.

Just before the turning on the left into Guildhall Street the photographer stands in the middle of the road to capture this leisurely scene of Edwardian Grantham. It appears the worst that can befall him is a collision with the man on the cycle who seems more interested in Kinloch's wine stores than looking where he is going.

The offices of W.H. Garton, coal and coke merchants, were situated on the High Street opposite the top of Guildhall Street and here their cart can be seen decorated with a model coal mine, presumably to take part in a parade or procession. The building has long been demolished and the site is now occupied by Adams children's wear.

It looks like the decorators are in at Garrett's the drapers, who occupy part of Waterloo House in this scene from the 1920s. The shop between Garrett's and the George Hotel was the long-established ironmongers firm of Slater and Padget, later Gorin's tobacconists and confectioners. It became the home of Westmoreland's electrical goods for a time before Waterloo House was demolished in 1985.

In this 1912 postcard a car can be seen outside the High Street garage of George Whipple. George also had a department store in Watergate and when this burnt down during the First World War it was rebuilt as a garage and the business transferred to these premises. To the right of the garage was the butcher's shop of William Steel and on the corner of Finkin Street the premises of Wilkinson and Taylor whose products included leather goods and sporting equipment. On the opposite corner two borough workmen are repairing the road outside the printers shop of Leayton and Eden. The tailors, Dixon and Parkers, on the extreme right had recently moved from Butchers Row.

Telegrams—WHIPPLE'S GARAGE, GRANTHAM.   Telephone 102.   **17, HIGH STREET,**

GRANTHAM,   191

(Opposite the "George" Hotel.)

Dr. to G. WHIPPLE & SON,

Official Repairers to the Automobile Club of G.B. & I.

MEMBERS OF THE M.T.A.

Mr Senescal

Rover Cars.   Ritz Light Cars.   Diamond Motor Cycles.
Overland Cars.   Calthorpe Cars.   Rover Motor Cycles.
Ford Cars.   Harley-Davidson Motor-Cycles.

New MSU gear part	1	12. 6
carriage	1	10
2 new piston rings		5
Taking down & fitting		7
£	2	6. 4

RECEIVED WITH THANKS
WHIPPLE & SON,
MOTOR WORKS,
GRANTHAM.

Oct 16/15

According to this billhead of 1915, Whipple's garage was the agent for several makes of machine in the early days of the motorcar. It claims to represent names now long forgotten and some still in business today. Note the Harley Davidson connection: how many of those were travelling up and down the streets of Grantham in this era?

		18, HIGH STREET,			
M.R.	Mr Baskir	GRANTHAM, July 1896			

Bought of W. STEEL,

(LATE WISEMAN & STEEL),

BUTCHER, GAME AND VENISON DEALER.

1896			
June 24	Steak 15		11½
25	Steak 15	1	4
27	M. Steak 1½	1	6
29	Chop 3/4		9
30	Suet 11		5½
	Loin Beef 4 10 9	3	6
	G. Beef 15		10½
July 3	Liver		6
4	Loin Chop		6
6	Lamb Chop 1	1	0
"	Lamb Chop ½		6
8	China Beef 4½ 9	3	4½
14	Beef 1¼		10
	Loin Lamb 5 12	5	3
16	Suet		3½
17	G. Beef 1		8½
21	G. Beef 1 6		9
	Suet 10		5
22	China Beef 6 3 9	4	8
23	Beef 1 3		9½
24	C. Liver 1 10	1	1
		£1	12.0½

The food mentioned on this William Steel billhead should certainly make the mouth water.

This view of Briggs and Gambles' chemists shop from the turn of the twentieth century was produced to advertise their business but soon after it was issued on a postcard the premises were bought by the Midland Bank. The building disappeared altogether when it was demolished to make way for the Marks and Spencer's store in 1933. Note how the curved frontage matches the building at the top of Finkin Street, suggesting that it had all been part of a long forgotten plan to complement the George Hotel, which was almost in the middle of the two on the opposite side of the road.

This scene of the decorations for the Coronation of George V in June 1911 shows Chambers' new premises with the windows boarded up, waiting for the glass to be fitted. Chambers occupied several locations in the town and had been in business since the mid-1800s trading as drapers, milliners and dressmakers. The department store was officially opened on 19 September 1911. On the right is the doorway of the Maypole dairies, which until recently still had its original shop fittings.

When this early postcard was produced in the late 1890s the far left of the Angel Hotel was a recent expansion of the premises: only a year or two before this had been the general stores of Edward Dickinson. Known as the Noah's Ark, this shop closed in 1891 and the Angel Hotel acquired the buildings and incorporated them into their own. To the right of the Angel is the boot shop of Hoskins & Sons, which had originally been the home of the wealthy Seckers family and in one room had a panel bearing the date 1611. This building was demolished in 1897 and the site redeveloped for Boots the chemists in the early 1900s. These premises are now occupied by a building society.

In this view of the Angel Hotel the beginning of Vine Street can be seen. Just visible round the corner is the printers and stationers of Thomas Palmer and on the left of the photograph is D.R. Sharpley's drapers and milliners shop. Sharpley had taken over the premises from Samuel Dawson at the turn of the century. The building, which was originally a seventeenth-century town house, was demolished in 1948 as part of the Watergate road-widening scheme.

In 1887 the country celebrated the golden jubilee of Queen Victoria's reign and here we see the celebration arch which the Grantham people erected at the top of Watergate. The draper's shop on the right (referred to above) was occupied by Samuel Dawson who moved into the premises in the 1870s.

Ten years later and this time the celebration is for the Queen's diamond jubilee. The Queen did not get an arch this time but there were plenty of decorations all the way down Watergate.

When King Edward VII was crowned in 1902 the top of Watergate again displayed a fine arch together with an abundance of garlands and flags. This photograph was taken in June but the King was taken ill and the actual Coronation was postponed until August. It had been more than half a century since the country had seen a Coronation and the population of Grantham were determined to make the most of it. By now Dawson had been replaced by Sharpley, who occupied the premises until their demolition just after the Second World War.

Whichcote House in Watergate was originally a private Georgian dwelling but here, in the first decade of the twentieth century, it is one of the business premises of Chambers and Co. For many years prior to this it was occupied by a tailor called John Burgin. When this view was taken only half of the frontage had been converted to a shop window and the building still had a fine front door with a stone arch above.

By late 1911 Chambers had moved to their new premises on High Street and now Whichcote House is occupied by the well-known firm of Halfords. They came to Grantham in 1913 and extended the shop frontage to include another window to the south of the entrance. Cycling was already extremely popular in the early 1900s and there were several shops in Grantham catering for cyclists needs, however Halfords was the first nation-wide store to come to town and soon started to take a large share of the market.

This is Watergate in the 1920s and almost all the buildings in this scene have been swept away by the march of progress. All that remains are the premises on the extreme left of the picture.

This postcard was sent in 1956 and shows the results of the first stage of the plan to widen Watergate.

12 and 13, WATERGATE,

GRANTHAM, *Sept.* 190*8*

Mr J Senscall

Bot. of **HENRY COLLARD**

(GRANTHAM AND LONDON),

General and Furnishing Ironmonger,

ELECTRIC BELL-HANGER AND GASFITTER,

Agricultural Implement Merchant,

CHINA and GLASS MERCHANT, and SPORTS OUTFITTER.

STOVES, GRATES, and KITCHEN RANGES of every description.   Experienced Workmen sent to all parts of the County.

TELEGRAMS—COLLARD, GRANTHAM.   TELEPHONE 3Y4.   LONDON BRANCH—COLLARD & CO., 264, LAVENDER HILL, S.W.

100 Sporn Cartridges	7	10
Paid. Sept. 21/08		

The author's first job after leaving school in 1959 was as an errand boy at this shop down Watergate. It was one of the last true ironmongers in the town, where customers could buy anything from a tin-tack to a garden gate. Old ladies would come into the shop and ask for glass chimneys for their oil lamps and sure enough they were usually in stock on the top floor. Still packed in the straw they were delivered in goodness knows how many years ago. This billhead of 1908 shows the shop in all its glory but by the 1950s the ground floor portion on the right had been occupied by Whipple's, who ran it as a record shop. The business closed in the 1980s and after alterations to its frontage, the building became a restaurant.

The butcher's business of Amos and Shepherd was situated on the east side of Watergate at Nos 33 and 34. This scene, taken outside their premises around 1905, has thirteen staff on view and suggests that they were one of the main meat dealers in the town at this time.

Seven

Finkin Street and the Castlegate Area

Much has already been written about Grantham's Saint Wulfram's church and its history is well documented. However a book on the town would not be complete without at least a mention of this majestic building. This postcard, postally used in 1910, shows the south-east prospect of the building.

In 1905 this postcard was sent as a Christmas greeting by Dr and Mrs Patterson to friends in Brant Broughton. Dr Patterson was the last in a long line of surgeons to live at what was then No. 11 Finkin Street but is now more well known to most Grantham people as Elmer House, on the corner of Elmer Street South and Finkin Street. Within a few short years of the photograph being taken, this fine façade was lost forever when ten feet of frontage was added. The extension can be clearly seen as the old building is of stone whereas the addition is of yellow brick. The premises were occupied for many years by Escritt and Barrel but are now used by the Kesteven Blind Society.

WESLEYAN CHAPEL - GRANTHAM.

Standing on the corner of Elmer Street South, the photographer has captured this quiet moment in 1910 showing the Methodist chapel in Finkin Street. The Blue Cow public house can also be seen at the junction with Castlegate.

A view of the Blue Cow public house in Castlegate at the junction of Finkin Street. This is now the site of the entrance to a supermarket. The cobbled pathways across the roads, clearly seen in this view, were a common sight before the roads were metalled.

A south-facing view in Castlegate. The three little girls with their shopping baskets are about to enter the grocer's shop of Thomas Smith on the corner of East Street, but like the other children in the picture, they were only too willing to stop and pose for a photograph.

North-facing views of Castlegate were favoured more often by the early photographers, mainly because they wished to include two of Grantham's more famous buildings in one photograph; the parish church and the public house with the living sign – a beehive.

An early view of the Beehive public house, taken when there were few leaves on the tree holding the living sign and therefore giving the photographer a clear sight of the beehive. The image was taken by Fred Fisher, Grantham's first photographer and is on what was termed as a 'carte de visite'. Fred opened his first premises on the High Street in 1854 and moved to London Road in 1872. On the reverse of this card Fred advertises himself at his first studio on High Street, dating the photograph to no later than 1872.

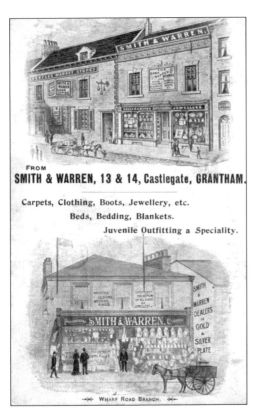

FROM
SMITH & WARREN, 13 & 14, Castlegate, GRANTHAM.

Carpets, Clothing, Boots, Jewellery, etc.

Beds, Bedding, Blankets.

Juvenile Outfitting a Speciality.

→ WHARF ROAD BRANCH. ←

The pawnbrokers Smith and Warren had two shops in Grantham in the early years of the twentieth century; one was on the corner of Brewery Hill and Wharf Road and the other at 13 and 14 Castlegate. This advertising postcard shows both their premises and was posted in 1903. The Wharf Road shop is now occupied by a firm selling electrical goods but in the skylight above the door is still displayed the words 'cash advanced' in leaded glass. When this postcard was sent there were three public houses within a very short distance of the Castlegate shop: the Beehive, the Star and Garter and the Rifle Volunteers. Smith and Warren's would be very handy if you found yourself in Castlegate with an uncontrollable thirst and no money in your pocket.

It was not always expensive items such as watches or jewellery that were pawned, often it would be mundane articles like boots, the Sunday suit or perhaps a favourite shawl. This ticket, now long redeemed, records that Mr Dawson of Middlemore Yard received 5s 6d when he pawned a pair of shoes.

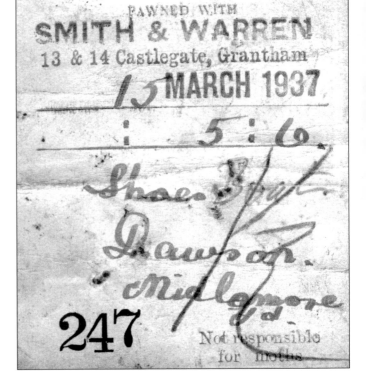

Eight

The Manthorpe Road Area

There has been little change in New Street on the right of this view, but since the photograph was taken in 1905 all the buildings on the left have completely disappeared. The cameraman has arrived in time to catch the local children on their way to school.

The children have again turned out for the photographer, this time in Sidney Street around 1910. Apart from the present day abundance of traffic this street has seen little change over the years.

The oldest part of the Kings School is the old schoolhouse in Church Street which was built in 1528. There have been several additions since and this postcard shows the official opening of the first to take place in the twentieth century. The building, on the corner of Brook Street and Castlegate, was opened in December 1904 by Sir Oliver Lodge, the Principal of Birmingham University. The school's own cadet force, formed in September the same year, took part in the parade.

This is a slightly later view of the new buildings and shows more of the Castlegate frontage. Until late in the 1800s this site was occupied by the British School, but it closed in 1895 and the premises were purchased by the Kings School for £525. The lower floor was converted into a science laboratory in 1898 before being replaced by the present building.

BRITISH SCHOOL, GRANTHAM.

This is to Certify

THAT *John R Adams*

was examined by

HER MAJESTY'S INSPECTOR,

and passed in the *Fifth* Standard

on *14th Feb 1887*

Signed *D Burrell*

N. E. T. Co., LEEDS AND YORK, No. 2.

This examination certificate serves as a reminder of the British School's existence. It was awarded to John R. Adams in 1887 and was signed by his schoolmaster Mr D. Burrell.

William John Hutchins, the Kings School headmaster, is the gentleman with the fine beard sitting in the middle of the front row. He was head from 1887 to 1898 and, though a good academic, was much criticized for his running of the school. It was said that during his time in office the pupils lacked discipline and the premises were less than clean. A keen fisherman, he would often be seen wearing a hat with various artificial flies attached to its fabric by their hooks.

This group photograph dates from around 1905 and by now William Rogers Dawson has a firm hold on the rudder. The Revd Dawson is seen by many as the man who transformed the school into a more dynamic entity. He was very keen to include sports into the syllabus and the school cadet corps was formed during his time in office. Perhaps the most significant indication of his success is the increase in the number of boys attracted to the school while he was at the helm. When Hutchins left in 1898 there were 51 pupils on the register, by the time Dawson moved on in 1906 this had risen to 230. The Revd Dawson is sitting in the middle of the second row surrounded by his assistant masters and pupils. It is obvious that school uniform was not an issue in the early 1900s – there is even a sailor suit being worn by one of the smaller lads. The younger boys in the group would have been members of the preparatory class that Dawson established in 1901 for under-eights. Before moving on the reader should study how this scene has been set up for the camera. It appears to be constructed of several tiers of forms: look at the chap on the right of the top row, his foot is extremely close to the edge. One can but wonder what his parents had to say when he arrived home with his school photograph!

Alexander J. Tate was headmaster at the school from 1917 to 1931 and here we see him (in the centre, with the dog) with the school's Officer Training Corps in 1924.

MANTHORPE.ROAD.GRANTHAM.

Used postally in 1911, this postcard of Manthorpe Road shows Wand's grocers and general stores on the right. This shop and all the houses as far as the tall one behind the ladder have all now disappeared with the redevelopment of the area. On the extreme left of the view is the Three Crowns public house.

This view of Manthorpe Road in the early 1900s sends a message down the years to present-day observers of how life was lived before the motorcar and the microchip.

The River Witham has caused havoc in Grantham many times over the years and on this occasion in 1910 the sender of the postcard, who lived in Redcross Street, says although her house was not affected, some people living in Alford Street had to move upstairs to escape the water. In this scene the flooded area is in-between the river and Manthorpe Road. Belton Lane bridge is to the right of centre among the trees.

The first stone of the town's General Hospital on Manthorpe Road was laid by Lady Brownlow on 29 Oct 1874. Erected at a cost of £5,000, the buildings were officially opened by Lady Brownlow on 5 Jan 1876. This view dates from around 1910 when it would have been impossible to envisage how big the complex was to become.

Turn off Manthorpe Road into Slate Mill Place and the traveller comes to this bridge at the entrance to Wyndham park. The bridge is on the site of the old Slate Mill which burnt down in the early 1890s. The old bridge was damaged in the 1922 floods and this one was constructed to coincide with the official opening of the park in 1924.

This is a view taken from the bridge in the previous photograph and shows the entrance to the swimming baths in Wyndham park. The park was opened on 10 July 1924 by Lady Leconfield whose son, Capt. Wyndham, was killed in the great war. Although the park is named after the captain, it stands as a memorial to all Grantham men who lost their lives in the conflict.

Wyndham Park, Grantham. No. 2925.

When this postcard was sent in 1926 the park had only been open for two years and there were still one or two farm buildings standing near the children's paddling pool.

GRANTHAM SWIMMING BATHS.

These were the days when men were men and their bodies had to endure the rigours of unheated, outdoor swimming baths. Many locals knew these baths as the Wyndham park swimming pool, but they were in existence long before the park got its name. Work on their construction was started in March 1886 and they were officially opened in July the same year. They were built by ninety-three unemployed men of Grantham and were designed by S.G. Gamble the Borough Surveyor. The total cost of the project amounted to £700, which included dressing sheds, caretakers hut, pegs and seats. The baths closed in the early 1970s.

Nine
Belton Lane, Military Camps and Hall's Hill

A peaceful setting showing Harrowby Mill still in working order around the turn of the century. The mill, situated on Belton Lane, dates back several hundred years but George Willoughby bought the business in 1907 and it is with his name that most locals identify the property. George worked the mill until his death in the early 1920s and it closed soon after.

The entire staff of Grantham's Steam Laundry on Belton Lane pose for the camera sometime just before the First World War. Many of the staff seen here would have lived behind the building in Laundry Cottages. The laundry was built in 1878 and remained on this site for more than 100 years, moving to new premises in Swing Bridge Road in 1989. When the old buildings were demolished the stone inscription above the main doors was incorporated on the company's new site. The original date stone of 1878 did not survive, however, and a modern replacement was substituted.

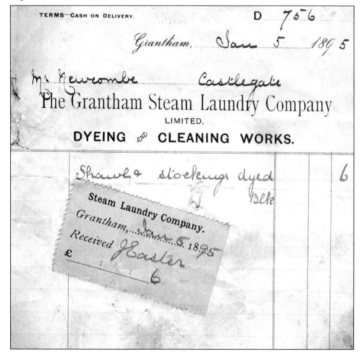

A billhead for the Grantham Steam Laundry proclaiming that the company undertook dyeing as well as cleaning. It shows that Mr Newcombe of Castlegate took advantage of this service and had a shawl and a pair of stockings dyed for the princely sum of 6d.

This scene shows the removal, in 1898, of the ancient stone bridge that crossed the River Witham on Belton Lane. It was replaced by a cast-iron, single-span bridge which had the width to cater for the increased traffic of the day and lacked a central pillar, a feature on several old local bridges at this time. Many locals held this pillar partly responsible for the floods that were a constant problem for the community. It must be said, however, that after this bridge and others like it in the town were replaced, flooding remained a problem in Grantham.

Taken from a static balloon, this scene shows a fair in full swing in the early years of the First World War. It is situated on part of what was Harrowby Army camp and towards the top of the picture a cluster of trenches used for training the raw recruits in the art of modern warfare can be seen. The ribbon of road snaking up to the top left-hand corner is what we know today as Hill Avenue, so named after one of the senior officers at the camp.

Harrowby was the smaller of the two camps situated on this side of Grantham, Belton Park being the larger of the pair. This scene, the first of three taken in 1936, shows the remains of one of the camp's boundary gates with the cameraman standing in Sandon Road, looking across Hill Avenue towards Gorse Rise.

Another gate, this time looking down Hill Avenue from New Beacon Road. A rough outline of Harrowby camp would start at the junction of Hill Avenue, run along Belton Lane, turning right up Harrowby Lane and running along close to the base of Halls Hill before turning back down to the Hill Avenue junction with Belton Lane.

The final photograph of the three shows what was left of the gates on New Beacon Road. The view looks towards Beacon Lane with the cameraman standing a few yards in front of the junction with Hill Avenue.

The infrastructure created for the Harrowby camp was put to good use between the wars when the town council built many homes in the area, firstly to replace dwellings condemned in the town during the 1930s and also to house part of Grantham's growing population. This scene shows the bottom of Uplands Drive under construction in 1936 with Nos 2 and 4 being the block of two houses left of centre.

Belmont Grove, off Uplands Drive, was also built in 1936 and this scene shows the group of houses almost completed with some of the families already in residence.

Many towns throughout the country have an elevated area that has been the site where, in times past, a bonfire was to be lighted to warn of impending hostilities or emergencies. Grantham is no exception; the particular high ground being Halls Hill. In more recent times the site has been used more for celebration than a forewarning of doom and this scene shows workmen building the celebration bonfire for the Coronation of George V in 1911.

Another view of the 1911 bonfire, this time completed and being guarded by a contingent of Grantham Boy Scouts.

The bonfire for George V's Silver Jubilee in 1935.

Lord and Lady Brownlow light the 1935 Silver Jubilee fire.

Two years later, in 1937: another Coronation bonfire takes shape, this time for George VI.

Another view of the 1937 bonfire, this time with a few young onlookers to make sure the older generation are doing it right.

CHURCH. PARADE. BELTON. PARK. 1911.

It is because of the First World War that many people connect Belton Park with the military but the Lincs. Yeomanry used the estate's parkland for their training exercises many years before the vast army camp was established. Here we see a church parade in 1911 that is well attended by both soldiers and civilians.

Soon after war was declared the training camps of Belton and Harrowby were taking shape. At first the troops in Belton camp lived under canvas but by the end of 1914 most of the soldiers were housed in wooden barracks, built by men like this group of joiners from Middlesborough.

114

A view of the camp early in the First World War showing both types of accommodation still in use.

Time for a bit of relaxation – these soldiers take five minutes' rest under the arch of Belmont Tower, which was built on heights within the park.

One type of postcard that the soldiers could buy to send home to their families and friends, this was termed a novelty card where the flap would lift up to reveal a ribbon of local views.

The YMCA played an important part in the army camps of the First World War and here we see Lord Kinnaird, president of the association, opening one of the new huts at Belton camp in 1915. This particular hut was paid for by the people of Manchester as at this time the camp was the home of many Manchester troops in the 11th Northern Division.

Y.M.C.A. No. 1 Hut. Belton Park.

The huts were very popular with the soldiers, many of whom had never been far from home before joining the King's army. The YMCA recognized how important it was that these troops, no more than boys in many cases, had somewhere they could go to relax, play a game of cards or darts, write a letter home or just spend some time away from the everyday atmosphere of military life. This group pose for the camera outside hut No. 1.

Y.M.C.A. No. 2 Hut. Belton Park.

The interior of YMCA hut No. 2 shows it equipped with a well-stocked canteen, a piano and on the right of the picture its own post office. This postcard was sent in 1917 and by now the machine-gun corps are at the camp and the soldier sitting with his elbow on the table has the corps badge on his hat.

KID LEES 24TH MANRS V McEWAN SOUTH LANCS AT GRANTHAM JULY 3TH 1916

This is where I am just now.

BELTON PARK

I'm still "on the map" you see !

A.J.C.—288

Boxing matches between the troops were another form of relaxation and by the size of this crowd a very popular one. Even the photographer has abandoned his camera to get a better view.

A postcard sent by Ted Morris to his father who lived in Stratford-upon-Avon. The postcard is a light-hearted attempt to give families an idea where their menfolk were carrying out their military training. The date of the postcard is June 1916 and Ted states on the back that he expects to be 'sent over' towards the end of the week. This message makes one wish that Ted made it back from 'over there' to be reunited with his family in Warwickshire.

Ten
Barrowby Road, North Parade and Northwards

A scene not easily recognized in present-day Grantham, this area at the bottom of Barrowby Road is no longer the quiet avenue of trees depicted on this postcard of the early 1900s. It has undergone a considerable amount of change since the local milkman could leave his churns in the shade of a convenient tree while perhaps delivering his wares to the houses at nearby Mount Pleasant.

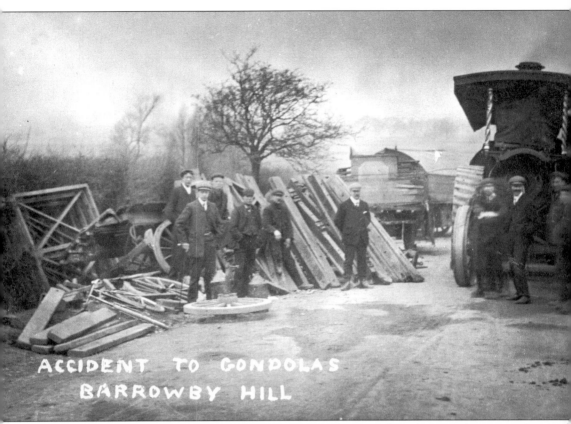

ACCIDENT TO GONDOLAS
BARROWBY HILL

Fred Savage's Gondola ride was a regular visitor to the Grantham fair and this scene, dated around 1910, shows the aftermath of an accident on Barrowby Hill in which the dismantled apparatus parted company from its conveyance. The photographer on hand to record the aftermath was Walter Wheeler whose business premises, called Bon Marché were at 51 High Street. He started out as a musical instrument dealer but changed track and turned his shop into a fancy repository, also running a confectionery business next door at No. 50. Photographic postcards by Wheeler are rare but he did publish many printed cards including several of the Grantham rail crash and the Somerby Hill carrier's accident.

Although this postcard of 1918 states that it is a view of North Parade, it also shows a small portion of North Street with this fine row of town houses on the right culminating at the butcher's shop of Vale and Son on the corner of Broad Street.

We leave Grantham as we entered the town, on the Great North Road. This peaceful scene on North Parade dates from around 1910.

The population of Gonerby Hill Foot has increased considerably since this photograph was taken in the 1930s. The houses on the left of the view are in Pretoria Road, Kimberley and Ladysmith Terraces, all names relating to towns in South Africa, which was the arena for the Boer War of 1899-1902.

Another 1930s view of Gonerby Hill, this time looking south towards Grantham. Lee and Grinlings were still going strong and their No. 14 maltings can be seen behind the first telegraph pole from the right.

The original Great Gonerby School dates back to 1841 but this group stands in front of the buildings erected in 1872 when it was enlarged. It was first called The National School but in 1905 the name changed to The Public Elementary. The pupils and staff in this picture posed for the cameraman at the turn of the century when Edward Lloyd Davies was headmaster and Miss Emma Lupton the senior mistress.

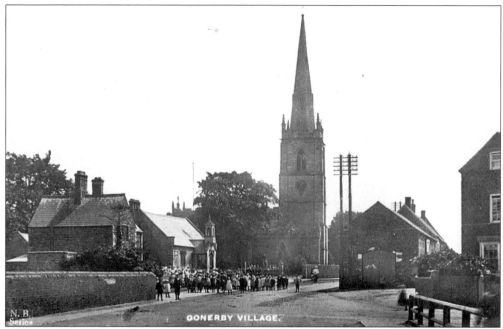

Sent in the second decade of the 1900s, this postcard of Great Gonerby shows the church of Saint Sebastian and a thriving village school. The railings on the right are alongside the village pond, which has now long since been filled in.

These determined looking gentlemen are players and officials of the 1908/9 Great Gonerby football club team.

The High Street in Great Gonerby at the time of this view, around 1910, was also part of the Great North Road. It is an example of traffic congestion in the 1900s.

A scene in Great Gonerby off the main road in Green Street around 1905. This view has changed little today, almost a century later.

Parker's had been in business in Great Gonerby since the second half of the nineteenth century and this photograph, taken around 1910, shows their staff assembled outside the front of the bakery on the village High Street.

Before Long Bennington was bypassed in the late 1960s, it was the last village in Lincolnshire when travelling north that had the Great North Road as its main road. Soon after leaving this community the highway entered Nottinghamshire to continue its journey to Scotland. This north-facing view dates from the first quarter of the twentieth century.

The building covered in creeper in this 1920s scene was the home of W.S. Barnes' general store. Now it houses both the village post office and a fish and chip shop.

On the right of this south-facing scene, taken between the wars, the old school that was replaced by the present buildings in April 1984 can be seen. The original Long Bennington village school was erected in 1847 and stood on part of the present school's playground. The garage on the left of the scene was replaced in the 1950s by a more modern service station. This in turn was demolished and the site used for the erection of the two bungalows that stand there today.

THE CEMETERY.

It is often stated by postcard collectors that almost anything can be found on one if you look long and hard enough. This one of Grantham cemetery helps to support this assumption. Imagine sending this postcard at the turn of the century to one's nearest and dearest, the message on the back might read, 'Arrived safely yesterday, weather fine, this area of town is very quiet as the neighbours keep to themselves, wish you were here.'

Acknowledgements

While working on this book I have met and talked with many people in an attempt to clarify information or fill in the odd date. Every one of them, without exception, were more than willing to help in whatever way they could and I take this opportunity to thank them all for their assistance, especially Mr Sid Duller whose knowledge of local history, often of the unwritten kind, has helped at times to give life to the book. I would also like to thank the staff of the Grantham library who made the necessary research that much easier with their help and patience. No pictorial history book would be possible without the endeavours of the early photographers and I take great pleasure in acknowledging all those that are known to have produced images that appear in this book. These are: Fred Fisher, Alfred Emery, Walter Lee, H. Bliss, F.G. Simpson, Walter Wheeler, George Scothern, Frank Urwin, Tuson, I. Cross and T.H. Bennett. Last, but by no means least, I thank my wife Jenny who has spent many hours gathering information and has helped with the layout and compilation of this book.